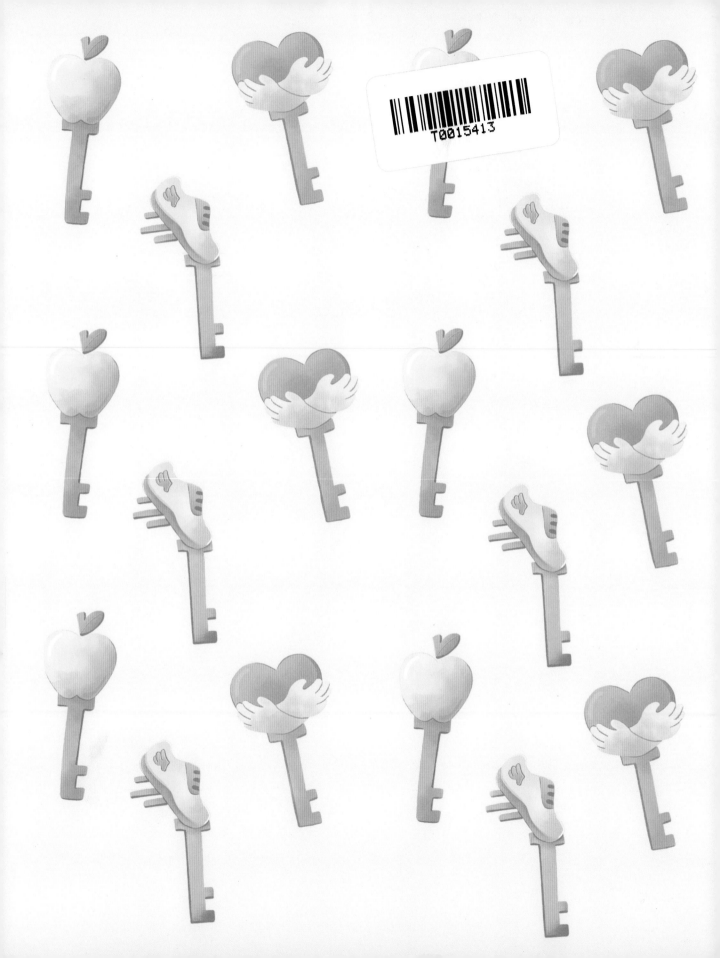

Dedicated to Chris Burke—
daddy, husband, hero.
You will always hold the keys to our hearts.

This is the first book for mother-daughter writing duo Chloe (daughter) and LaRanda (mom).

In 2019 at twenty-one years old, Chloe had open-heart surgery to fix a rare congenital heart defect. The journey from discovery to diagnosis to her life-saving surgery was long, painful, and scary, but Chloe's light only grew brighter.

She is a passionate advocate with the American Heart Association and is on a mission to help people, especially women and children, protect their hearts by making simple changes to improve their heart health.

That mission inspired this book.

MASCOT
KIDS!
an imprint of Amplify Publishing Group

www.mascotbooks.com

KEYS TO YOUR H. E. A. R. T.

For more information, please contact:
Mascot Kids, an imprint of Amplify Publishing Group
620 Herndon Parkway #320
Herndon, VA 20170
info@mascotbooks.com

CPSIA Code: PRKF0123A
Library of Congress Control Number: 2023902095
ISBN-13: 978-1-63755-754-9

Printed in China

Keys to Your
H. E. A. R. T.

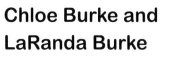

Chloe Burke and
LaRanda Burke

Illustrated by
Samantha Jo

BIG or small, short or **tall**,
for one and for all,
one thing is true
for **me** and for **you**.

We all have a **HEART**,
and treating it well is very,
very smart.

What does it **mean** to treat your heart well?

I'm glad you asked, for we'd **love** to tell!

There are *three keys* to unlock a healthy heart;
they don't cost much money, but you **must** do your part.

In fact, these keys are quite **simple** to use,
even ***easier*** than tying your shoes.

The first key is healthy eating, which is really just feeding yourself . . .

the
right
foods

in the
right
way

and in
the right
portions to fuel
how you play.

fruits   grains

veggies   protein

dairy

The servings you need depend on your **age** and **size**, so eating the size that's right for you is **very wise**.

Lean protein, fruits, and veggies; low-fat dairy and whole grains are the foods that we need to **power** our bodies and brains.

Foods with added sugar, salt, and fat can taste really yummy,
but too much is **bad,** so it's best to not put them in your tummy.

Eat **more** of the good foods and **less** of the bad!
It's the **smart** way to eat, and your heart will be **glad**.

For key number two, it's aerobics you're after:

these are the activities that make your heart **beat** faster.

Exercise is good, at least sixty minutes a day.
Get off of the couch—

go **outside** and **play!**

To get your heart **pumping**,
there's so much you can **do**.

You can **walk**,

skip,

run,

ride a bike,

or **hop** like
a kangaroo!

If the weather is **bad** or you're **stuck** indoors,
play games like **hide-and-seek** or have a **dance party**,
of course.

You're a kid, so have **fun**—it isn't a chore
to play games with your **friends** and move your body more.

Key three is reduce tension—a big word for stress—which is a **pressure** you feel in your **head** and your **chest**.

It can be caused by **change**, **fear**, or **pain**—
things that make your heart **pound** and **worry** your brain.

Feeling bad or being scared **isn't** weak or wrong;
it only hurts your heart when it stays **too** long.

Good news, there are things you can do
for a **happier heart** and a **happier mind,** too.

Try these **stress busters** to help **reduce tension.**
Share your fears with someone you trust who will listen.
Get plenty of sleep—at **least** eight hours a night.

It's hard to

L A U G H

and be stressed,

so laugh with **ALL**

of your **might.**

Listen to music,

play a game,

pet a dog or a cat;

do things

that make you happy,

it's as simple as that.

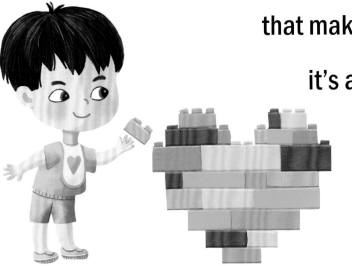

Now that you have the **keys** to your heart,
open the lock, **take** a step—
that is your **part**.

As you begin your journey, keep this in mind:
laugh often; do good; to yourself and to others, **be kind**.

Eat well, move more, stress less—that's the start
for improving the health of your **sweet** little heart.

RESOURCES

We found these online resources helpful when writing this book. If you need help, we encourage you to talk to your child's pediatrician, school counselor, or others with the expertise to give you guidance.

The American Heart Association, www.heart.org, has great resources for all three keys to heart health for the whole family.

HEALTHY EATING:

USDA
myplate.gov/

Smithsonian Science Education Center
ssec.si.edu/pick-your-plate

HealthyChildren.org
healthychildren.org/English/ages-stages/gradeschool/nutrition/Pages/Making-Healthy-Food-Choices.aspx

FUN AEROBIC ACTIVITIES:

Tiny Beans
tinybeans.com/games-and-activities-to-get-kids-moving/

Seattle Children's Hospital
pulse.seattlechildrens.org/indoor-active-play-for-heart-health/

CNet
cnet.com/health/parenting/fun-games-to-get-your-kids-to-exercise/

Connecticut Children's Hospital
connecticutchildrens.org/cardiology-cardiac-surgery/23-indoor-activi-ties-for-heart-healthy-kids/

REDUCING TENSION AND STRESS:

Kids Health
kidshealth.org/en/parents/stress.html

Psychology Today
psychologytoday.com/us/blog/dont-worry-mom/201302/12-tips-reduce-your-childs-stress-and-anxiety

Mayo Clinic
mayoclinichealthsystem.org/hometown-health/speaking-of-health/the-art-of-kindness